AF597421

More praise for RADIAL BLOOM

"What if the Muse arrives 'all biceps and brawn... in a leather jacket of disinterest,' holding a golden gun he puts to your heart? In this potent fever-dream of a conceit, Amy Ratto Parks not only radicalizes the paradigm, she enacts the brutal consequences, both existential and quotidian, of responding to the call. Classically speaking *Radial Bloom* is a descent, an urgent journey into the interior that is never top-heavy – imagine Julian of Norwich, Baudelaire, and John Wayne sitting at the bar with Dante pouring shots – and is impossible to put down."

~ Chris Dombrowski, author of *Body of Water*

"The remaking of the self – be it through mania, depression, obsession, or heartache – can be an otherworldly experience, rendered here in *Radial*

Bloom as a cinematic and transcendent act. For those of us tucked safely into a life that has been domesticated by a partner or children, there is the tendency to wonder where that person we were before has disappeared to. We wonder not about long-gone pleasures, but about longing itself, a kind of yearning that attended and sustained us for years with its sweet, familiar pain. The answer is that it's all still there, inside us, like it's always been. A lingering ache in the gut, a punch that still reverberates like distant thunder on a cloudless day. Amy Ratto Parks is the antidote to the part of us that reflexively dismisses our more complicated selves. This book is her big middle class, mid-life, multi-layered, mommy middle finger raised high, and I will follow it anywhere, especially right off this safe little cliff I've been perched on for years."

~ Keetje Kuipers, author of *The Keys to the Jail*
and editor at *Poetry Northwest*

RADIAL BLOOM

a mosaic novel by

AMY RATTO PARKS

Folded Word
Meredith, New Hampshire

ISBN: 978-1-61019-239-2

Folded Word
79 Tracy Way
Meredith, NH 03253
United States of America
WWW.FOLDEDWORD.COM

98765432 FIRST PRINTING

This book is for you, reader.
(It is also your story.)

CONTENTS

ACKNOWLEDGEMENTS

Thank you to John Sibley Williams for the book's title and for finding it a home. Thank you to JS Graustein, Zakariah Johnson, Barbara Flaherty, and the team at Folded Word for shepherding this book into being. Thank you to Natalie Peeterse and Claire Hibbs-Cheff for reading early (unwieldy, exhausting) drafts of this book and for seeing within it, something worth pursuing.

And my deepest gratitude to you, Russell, for your patience during the very intense period in which this book was written; you understood even when all of it was so beyond understanding. Thank you for always being my soft landing.

~ Amy Ratto Parks

RADIAL
BLOOM

He stuns you by degrees.

~ Emily Dickinson

we come to you directly
without touching

~ Lucille Clifton

PROLOGUE

Before you know the rest, you should know this: I live in a pleasant house on a quiet street in a modern-day Mayberry with mountains. I fell in love with my husband when I was still in my teens and now we have a daughter and a son, and a dog and a cat, and a handful of sturdy fish. We have cabinets of bright coffee mugs and chipped plates for our toast. Usually there are flowers on the kitchen table. Usually, music is playing. We have knick-knacks from trips to Vegas and photos of us smiling, thumbs-up on chairlifts over a white expanse of snow. We have closets full of vacuum cleaners and Soft Scrub and batteries and Super Glue. And a green yard and a brown fence and crabapple trees and maples and aspens. And a garage full of bike tires, scooters, sand buckets, rakes, ant poison, mouse traps, and long wooden boards, which, in the winter, we use to build an ice rink where the kids slide back and forth laughing in the snow. We hardly ever lock the house. In the summer, we all eat dinner together on the back porch where the full, thick leaves of the grapevines temper the evening sun.

We live a kind of privileged normalcy that most people don't believe is real. But all of this is real.

And so is this: Once there was a man who came to me and stayed. Or he had always been there and never left. Or he was a muse born of my prayers. Or he was my every shame or my every fear or my every love risen up in the shape of a man. Or he was a simple ghost trying to find the light. This is his story. And mine.

We met abruptly on the corner near the kids' school. He was running toward me, hand inside his jacket, searching for a weapon. I imagined a knife through my ribs – or a cord around my neck – but then he was so close to me and I was afraid and could not move and his hand rose from the black coat and there was a golden gun lifted in the air, and he fell toward me, plunging it through my chest and resting against my heart, gold against red, and the trigger went and I was exploded. I stood there on the corner. No one knew. And no one saw a thing.

I exploded and no one saw a thing? Is this possible? If you wonder, then you have never before fallen in love.

From the rhythm of my daily life he pulled me forward as if by hooks beneath the collar bones, and I followed step by step. I didn't want to follow but I wanted to follow. He haunted my children. Their voices echoed reaching far back into me where I sat at the end of the long hall of myself watching my life while I witnessed all of those sacred places invaded, washed over with him – *do you hear me* my children asked, but I – He was a blind man with a rope. He twisted into me. (I tried to wait for the wind to die down, but I fell as a dead body falls.)

Then he was everywhere. In the bath, in the car, in the park he came back to me in words *ein muss sein! ein muss sein!* came back to me quiet and dark-eyed, a secret I carried beneath my shirt. Was catalyst or synthesis or dilation: the seedpod broken open, fire-ruptured, the spore floating wayward, pulled through dark passages between us.

He was the feeling of a hand on my neck, a hand on my cheek, a hand on my hand on my face and that face and all of this – I wanted this – *ein muss sein, ein muss sein* – he was there and seemed impossibly alive. His own body breathed into me blowing smoke into the cold night, blowing warm breath against my breath, almost like rescue, almost like love.

At first, he showed me the selves he wanted me to see: he was an icon, a legend, an officer in uniform with a clean, square jaw. Was starched and stern and tasseled and badged. Be-gunned. Be-powered. Granted berth on a wide stage. Was on a horse. On a motorcycle. In a fast car. Hanging from a cliff. Was biceps and brawn. Cursing and cigars in a leather jacket of disinterest. He loomed massive against the horizon. Might as well have been wearing a holster and a Stetson saying *talk low, talk slow, and don't say too much* (yes sir) and crowing over the goddamn price of whisky to his boys. He was a man that all women loved, all men even, I thought. When we walked together, he was shameless with the eyes. That loping half smile. That habit of faux submission had remained and his presence was huge: every person he passed inflated, but he was always alone this one. Walked off, hands in the pockets. And the others scattered like disinterested fish.

Perhaps it sounds like it would have been horrible, but I wanted the words his presence brought. He came and I wrote. It was so simple. So I laughed and thought *thank God this man doesn't know I am stealing from him*. That I am the thief and the swindler. That I take the scalpel of him between my two fingers and hurl him across the green lawn, watch him spin toward the heads of my loved ones who stand there unblinking as the shining silver danger of him comes forward, end over end, and lands cleanly in the apple's flesh. Being near him was like throwing knives, throwing knives into trees.

And even so, I suppressed him imperfectly. I aimed for a steel-armed push-back, for a grenade-powered, shield-blocked, riot-ready stance. But he squeezed out from all the proper edges. Slid out from beneath my white linen Sunday dress, from beneath my PTA cookies, my golden mommy badge. He appeared while I was sharing a recipe or talking about my child's runny nose. From the perfect envelope of my life, he slid like a brown-eyed, smirking virus and said flatly — *wow.*

In the beginning, he rarely left. He watched me from the picture windows in my living room, sat above the fireplace, waited in the hot tub and shook his head. He was unimpressed by the fact of me emptying small cans full of used tissue, washing dishes in pink rubber gloves, packing tiny bags of blueberries for lunch. *How domestic*, he said.

He decided that he knew what was in my best interest. That somehow I had failed to honor our agreement, so he entered me by force. Created a command post. Sat in his sun-drenched, thatch-roofed hut, while I fanned him, brought him bourbon and ice. He made sure that I understand the new power structure. My skin pulled heavy on my face. He told me I was tired and I believed him. Then he blew out of me like bees, left me like an empty hive, a voice with no body, a word with no print. He told me to ask him if I needed to know what it felt like to be human.

It wasn't long before certain things became clear. He was a thief and a swindler, promised me the gun against his shoulder, the diamonds in his pockets, which turned to sand when I showed interest. Curled his lines around my wrist like a handcuff. Was almost always sick – heart broken, worn with cold, the child left for dead – hand to his rag belt, he'd say *how dare you leave me here?* Was unapologetic in his demands, wretched with neediness. Callous against my children, my husband. Cared nothing for what I could lose. Begged me off sleep, off food, off any single thing. Laid in bed between my husband and I, made love between us, snooped, ear to a glass behind the door of our most tender conversations. Begged to know my kids, made offers of giant stuffed pandas and live monkeys, clowns and glittering tiaras (he was smart that way, too) and he fought me fist to the chest when I kept them away, told him the time would come. Was shameless, greedy for me, was a wretched pig of a thing, and just when I considered welcoming him, just when I considered his demands for custody, his buyouts, his formal papers he turned and walked. Just like that. Down the boardwalk in the horizontal wind, snow on his collar, in his ear, and smiled back at me with cold, cold teeth.

He made me sit outside the house and wait until Andromeda had moved across my windshield in the night sky. He loped out of the house, towel in hand down the driveway, and I rolled down my window, returned his smile. He leaned in close, exhaled and said, *how did you find me?* Then, *I'm not ready to commit.* I stared at the stop sign on the street in front of me. I wasn't ready yet either, but I had been at this long enough that I didn't know if what I mean is *I'm not ready to wait* or *I'm not ready to drive away*. Then he was gone. Into thin air. *Thin air,* I thought, *is any air we fall through –*

I fell through and then things changed. I was changing, too. I grew gills and a fish's tail and I slicked myself between his two wide palms that once held food and now held only the sea. He only wanted to touch me, the novelty of my scales, the newness of this dimorphic *thing* that was suddenly curious about him. I turned my fish's body to look at him directly, our bodies perpendicular, he kneeling in the sandy shallows and I floating up, swimming with my face to his, and I opened my mouth and he saw the sunlit insides of me, the pink organs, the water flushing in and out, the steady white of my needle-bones, the red pulse of me (the red pulse), and he was breathing then too fast, and he lost his air, lost the use of those unevolved lungs, and I saw his eyes go big as disks before he bolted straight back up toward his own life. For the first time, he began to suspect that he would not always be able to find me, and that maybe I would bring him down again and again.

But I wanted this new version of myself, too, and he was just out of reach so I made offers: I would open my bones, arch my ribs onto their hinges, and make a place for him. I would close myself around him with messy stitches, punctured light entering the fleshy nest of me. Instead he was out there, flexing his elbows and knees, standing there at his full height, opening his palms wide toward me like a ball player. Like he was ready to either catch me or push me away.

So he had power, but he was not very useful. I had to remind myself of this. He couldn't flip an egg in the pan, clean a deer, build a car, or dissemble a bed. Couldn't bake bread in an open fire, or pull a man from a river. Was not a partner to me, didn't buy me plants or make my tea. Never had my health in mind. He didn't kiss me at night, didn't lie with his chest to my back and curl against me, didn't convince me (ever) to trust that he could save me from any sudden flood. Told me every day that I could not have him, that I was not smart enough to understand his jokes, beautiful enough to be on his arm. *Quick now, here, now, always,* he was the hidden laughter in the foliage that I couldn't stop chasing.

Once he was there it seemed that he had been there forever. Was there at my birth, watching my mouth on my mother's breast. Was there when my blood first streamed red beneath me. Was there when my father died, when I broke myself into the part in my bedroom and the part down below on the sidewalk. Was there when I was lost myself

in the woods and was there when I was birthing,
when I thought I would die, when I laid there on
the floor trying to break the egg of my voice out
into the air. Was there every time I'd punched
the wall, goading me, creaking out slim laughter,
saying *there you go, keep at it, look at you trying to be so tough.*

Then suddenly, he was smaller than I would have imagined. He was floating like a seed dispersed, like something broken loose of its core, like a shard of stratospheric ribbon: a leftover part of someone's long-forgotten mission that was blown through all the intermittent darkness, star energy, cosmic thrum, waiting for something with enough gravity to pull him in. I had misjudged the distribution of weight. I watched him try to catch me. Watched the muscles in his neck and legs strain. Watched his knees slowly bend straight to earth.

And then the square-jawed, Hollywood man was gone and I could not keep him sober, could not keep him out of the peyote buttons, the mescal, the mushrooms. *To hell with it all,* he said. I could not even convince him of the future, could not convince him of the possibility of regret. Loved him, in fact, for his dedication to *quick, now, here, now.* He blew past me like a plastic bag and I stomped down upon him, caught the thinnest edge of him beneath the heel of my boot, held him there while he struggled and I pointed to the torn skin on the edge of my fingers, pointed to the blood dried under the nail, up around the arc of cuticle, pointed out the brownish smear on the hem of my shirt and the taste of blood in my mouth. Told him this is what he did. That this was the wreckage: my consequence of him. He asked if I had a light. Excused himself to the porch and opened a beer. Told me, before I did anything else to step on inside and wash my hands.

It was clear then, that he was mine to protect. He was the orphaned ward granted to me and I holed him up, tried to explain the benefits of structure and discipline. He said nothing. Acted impervious. Acted as though he was just a drum belly I talked into where the words bounced like voices in a metal corridor. But I knew he had miscalculated his capacity for orbit. And he knew I didn't believe him. *Where are your wounds,* I asked him and he shrugged like he didn't know what I meant. *The bruises* – and I resisted the urge to bring him a poultice and cool cloths, to feed him ginger broth by the spoon, to make tea from tender leaves. He needed someone to touch his cheek, cup his chin and say *oh baby, it's ok,* and he was waiting there before me, gut opened and all, pretending I couldn't see the full picture. And I didn't have the nerve to say *no way in hell.* Couldn't throw a towel at him and say *cover yourself. Have some shame.*

Because I realized that he had become my story to tell. He was my character to dress, my marionette arms and legs and mouth to move. My show to perform. The voice for the monologue. The feet for the choreography. His calves and biceps were hand-picked. His eyes, his cheekbones had been chosen from hundreds. Initially, he was proud to be there: to be the lover on the balcony, the lover in the garden. The unrequited, the vengeful, the impassioned. The puffed-up bird of a man (the magpies, the crows). The waxy skinned. The unfractured. The scarless – but I dropped him and he fell, rag-dolled across me, and I stumbled out onto the stage. I left the safety of the heavy curtain, the dark jungle of props and pulleys and wigs, the comfort of the lines we had memorized.

(How could I explain this scene to the anonymous crowd? How could I atone for this?) The stage was wooden beneath my bare feet, and my own voice appeared, fell out before me: stillborn. Deep blue. Irretrievable.

The veil was gone and he hated me. He wore his pain like a bloody stomach wound and was shocked that I could see it pulsing there, through his shirt. He had made it that far believing that he would have to grant permission for this. But he was naked before me and was angry that I had not looked away, angry that I could not move my eyes from that backlit stomach fire – the explosion of self that bled openly. It had managed to sustain itself this long. It had fought off his body's attempts at both healing and further destruction. I stared until I could see it simply as a feature of him. Until I could see past the ugliness, past the thing I feared in him, the thing I would never touch, the thing that forced him open, made him vulnerable. *We're the same,* he said and pointed to my glass of whiskey. I didn't answer him. I considered the accusation. Considered my feet beneath me and reached down to find, yes, the earth there beneath me with its brown, unnoticeable curve. And then I looked up and he was gone.

While I weeded the garden, he stood leaning on the fence and smiled like there was a joke we shared, as though we had once spent an afternoon rowing a boat in the sun, or spent an evening together playing cards. I could see he was afraid of me: that his laughter was nervous, that his eyes were averted, but not out of coyness. I had something he needed and he was afraid I wouldn't give it to him – and yet, when he left, I always knew myself more. I realized that I had let him in, that I could get him out. That I never would. That I would not know my life. That I would not know –

He did not know that I was a thief by nature. He would look at me with gentle eyes and it made me want to pull that Catholic curtain closed and confess everything *(Lord Father, how I have sinned)*, outline all of the ways I had deceived him, tell him about this story I was stealing. But he had an improper idea of possession, and so I did not try to explain that these words were only his in the way the arch possessed the raven through it. Only the way the vase holds the lily. The catalyst does not

own the explosion (alchemy of spirit, grammar
of excess, texture of proximity) and I remembered
that the urge to confess had been bred in me. That
he was no innocent himself. That he had stolen
plenty from my life. And I didn't believe in sin.
And I didn't believe my own urge to false guilt.
So, I took from him as he took me apart. I looked
through the window of him and took only the best
pieces of myself.

Throughout all of this, I reminded myself that he was not my man. Was not the silvery net – fine as birth caul – that encased me at night, that reminded me that I would not drown, that I could breathe in all that water, that placed his hands on me holding me to earth. He was not the body that was my air, that entered and remade me. Was not the one that fed my body and reminded it to live here on the earth, on the shore where our feet could always land, and having landed, could move forward.

Instead, he and I made dates, but the timing never worked out. He would appear while I was in love with the image of my sleeping children (their hot pink cheeks, their soft lips pursed in dream, their shining hair) and I would motion madly at him to back off. Or I would show up at some bar and sit there at a table ordering drink after drink waiting for him, forcing myself to keep my eyes on the book I was reading, resisting the gravity of every passing stranger. I would force myself to look serious and interested in my own work as though my disinterest in him might be appealing. Sometimes it helped if I pretended he was really the one in charge – and finally his lazy, late self would walk in and I'd wait for him to cough up all of his thorny, ugly excuses. But he wouldn't. He'd tell me I came too early. Sat in the wrong booth. Ordered the wrong drink. Would tell me that by now I should know better.

And I did know better. It's not like he was a secret. It's not like he was hiding in the basement or jumping from a second story window when a car pulled into the driveway. He wasn't some visitor that showed up at Christmas. We all knew he was there: the whole family tiptoed around the fragile egg of him. Everyone had learned that it was better to just let him be when he'd decided to get onto me. The kids told me I was mean when I protected him. My husband got jealous. But we all gave in, shared the dinner table, passed him the salt when he asked. We all knew he had his own problems. Loved too much or not enough. Could not commit to anyone, got nervous when someone depended on him, and lied just to keep his own space.

Finally, one day, he was gone. Not just away for the moment, but the whole sense of him was gone and only the idea of him floated up through the stairwell of me: like a Halloran rhythm he peeled back into open echo. The breath, an elegant transistor. I held the tongue on the long bell of evening. I waited for the echo to end.

The strange contagion of him had made me forget the self of myself and this realization caught me at the throat. He was the bright dream-life of untold stories, of all those maps we never unfold because we fear taking roads that might never turn back. He seemed to care nothing for me, but still was the hand that lead me forward into this – he was my own confusing Beatrice or Virgil. He was prayer or breath (but impotent prayer, held breath). He was the hammer that fractured me (brute beauty), shattered me to glass splinter.

But he was not a magician, not a wizard, was not the kind of muse crowned in olive boughs. He did not trust me either (how many times had I left him?) and I demanded that he trust me no matter how many times I fell in love with others, no matter how many times I decided that I could do just fine (thanks) without him. But he stood at the periphery of my dreams and brought me back, and the quietest yellow corner of my soul said, *Manibus, oh, date lilia plenis.* (Dear god) come to me, with hands full, oh, give me lilies.

He would always come back, but never in the way I had hoped. His presence in my life was like the indefensible squalor of water that threatens a dam. Was a flood born of fear, of mistake. Flood of envy, heartache. The slums in the flood plain of my soul were washed by him: the trashy alleys, the rat-eaten mortar, all of it crumbling, all of it washed. I lived there knowing the consequence. Took the land given me and had never traded up. Never bartered for an inland refuge. Slept every night awaiting the wash — the rush, the final cough of death. Woke every morning breathing the air bent on my survival.

I knew by then that he could easily take me from my life, but I wanted to know: What would become of us in that clapboard house? How would those walls sustain all the things that would ineffably bear down? And if we could hold ourselves long enough, what would we see when we ascended the roof? What would remain above the water? Who would hold my hand and say *you always knew this was coming?*

He told me all of those questions were ridiculous. Said I'd been swimming all my life for it. That I had learned from the accidental inhales, the ill-timed attempts at breath. Claimed that I did not want land. Asked about the lead disks I kept in my pockets. Asked about the benefits of fast descent. Said to release the air and watch the world ascend past me like I was falling volcanic into the mouth.

There came a time when he left and I became the damp quiet. I could no longer return to the self I had been before him. I was something that had been spun in circles and dropped, disoriented in a field of hay down. My eyes were tired and the banter words between us were all water, all fluid falling. And I was falling: I was gravity's cold necessity. Eventually, he called but I did not answer and I wondered what he would do if I never answered. If he would turn inward and abandon me or if he would just continue to call into the grey air: *hello?*   *hello!* Perhaps he would he trail off or go out in virulent combustion while the perfect machine of me ground on in a different direction. My once-thick skin had become shell thin, tap-crackable.

All the other voices broke in and scattered me, spun the lens, like so many kinds of traffic.

When I got my bearings, I saw that he was on a dirt road in front of me, walking, swaggering into the sunset and I couldn't catch him, and he didn't even know I was not there next to him, didn't even know he was leaving me behind. I wanted to run after him but the air turned thick and gluey and my arms and legs became simple weights to be bared, and I wanted to be able to climb up into the viscous air and swim through it, swim past the clapboard farm houses and hold him by the arms and say *you have forgotten me,* and *how dare you,* and *you work for me, you bastard.* I wanted to be tough about it all. I wanted to bully my way back to him. But really, all I could do was sit on the sun-baked road and cry and hope that he could distinguish my cries from the cries of the birds above, from the cry of the wind, from the sting of the dirt blowing. Distinguish it even from the song he was humming: the tune he had. The words of which, of course, were me, were gone.

Then he was before me like a monument, his bare back shining like altar-glow, his attention elsewhere, and I wrapped my arms around the width of him. He could not imagine what brought me. Could not imagine why I would sit there holding him, my face against the skin of his back, binding him up with myself, with my small arms, my collar bones, my jaw line: all the smallness of me was holding him in place as though he might be prone to accidental ascension. As though suddenly his roots might break loose of the dry earth. As though I was the only small thing that had noticed in time, and grabbed hold of his thin and wind-tattered frame. As though, if I was not careful, we both could lift off like kites blowing endless through the ether.

Or he was at the end of a long hallway looking out the window. His back was to me, but I knew that he was waiting and I walked slowly, considering the best way to gain his attention. If I called his name, I risked startling him – like wild game – into a run. If I was too coy, he'd become bored and disappear. I could take his hand and lead him to the door or I could slip into the room and lure him back. But all of this is too indirect, unsatisfactory. Instead I approached him slowly, quietly, and slipped my hands under his sweater, ran them along the edge of his jeans. This worked. It earned me at least thirty minutes of affection: attention memory   grace. Then he was gone and I was there, knowing that I had been used for something beyond my own understanding. Knowing that this would happen again and again and again.

When he left, I would remember myself. I would lay naked in hot water under the stars moving over me and let myself inflate into other stories where he wasn't the central character. I would wash my face and go to sleep with my hair down. I was the dry stone (no sound of water) that slept all night in the yard. I was the car that sat like a slug in the driveway, and the sidewalk, flat as it was in the daylight, extended away from me around the boulevard. (The dancers were all gone under the hill. The houses were all gone under the sea.) I was rock covered in sand, covered in snow. Breathless, still. Only the slushing waves against my ribs: I was all the smooth stones, diminishing.

He and I swam under water in an August-warm pool. The chlorine burned our eyes and anonymous kids moved in a blur around us. I held onto the whale of him, tried to hold onto his slick shoulders, while he pulled the water with wide sweeps of his arms that lurched us forward through the scatter of bare legs and bright prints. And we were smiling. Silence and light cut the blue water, and all I wanted was this connection but the pounding of my held breath began breaking in my lungs and sent me swimming up. Above the water, as I opened my mouth to take in the quick air, he rose next to me, angry. He wanted to smack me and I didn't even know what I had done (didn't even know), but there was my face, and his bullet eyes at me, and his hand right there – stopped short.

He was like a pebble, a pearl that lived under my tongue in that place no one would ever touch with fingers, where my laughter washed over his curved back. I considered his various pasts: sea- or river-worn, tumbled and tragically washed for God knows how long. He was a bulb of promise, nacreous and luminary, where he sensed my words before they crossed my lips, where he navigated the shadowy channels I couldn't possibly see. He lived sometimes inside my cheek and he knew what was at stake: if he happened by some mishandling to land between my teeth, one of us would crack. We both agreed on symbiosis and made a promise against fracture.

Then we finally gave in to the stones in our pockets and we sank through the salt brine. Kelp twisted around our bare legs and loosened as we kicked gently to stay in place. All the people up there on the surface were smooth-bodied – all forearms and elbows – some floating in the pale blue cup of water, face-up to the sun; others lounging in row boats with parasols and pinafores. It was something charming.

And we were there below. Our hair floated up around our eyes set on them up there. We fluttered our hands to stay in place and said *stay with me here.* All we really wanted was land – some soft brown to sink into, something made to hold us: A cradle, a nest, something to rise up and grow from. But there were our fish eyes bulging up at those marionettes, and there was the sky broken by water, and there was the water – always the water – always the water waiting to drown us.

We settled into the institution of us. We sat on the floor and drew our fingers through the dust and looked across to take note of each other with the mutual curiosity of caged animals who, after years, continued to watch the other pacing, yawning, chewing bits of raw meat.

And more importantly, we agreed to softness. We agreed to attempt silence as a strategy. Agreed to quit brandishing our words, to release the scarred shields of our personas, our quivers of humor.
In truth, all of the tools of our evisceration were long dulled, and by then we were scar upon
scar, skin heaped up upon skin and tightening, binding across our torsos as evidence of these intimate wars. And there was nothing left to do but surrender to our untouchable distance, our tangible proximity.

We tossed a baseball at dusk. The white ball between us struggled to hold the fading light, to distinguish itself in the boundary-less, static light; and then a light snow began. We agreed that we should stop. That it was too hard to see. That we only knew the ball when it was suddenly a blare of red stitches too close –

We could have agreed to throw more gently. We could have agreed to different circumstance. We could have decided in fact, that the game itself was cliché, but that would have been a betrayal on its own: we both wanted to be there for the solid smack of the ball in the mitt, the hard knot of leather in the palm before release, the miracle of the light and the silent blind air for all those moments. All those moments before we knew for sure we'd made contact.

III

The turning point — if I can even fairly use that term here — was when he became worried about how everything might end. He could not think of an acceptable conclusion. Had so many logistical questions. I tried to reassure him. Told him that it was my job to get him out. That all he had to do is follow. I spread my papers out on the table, explained that there were always maps for this sort of thing: the tracks in the snow, the half-eaten kill. There was always a way to follow the ridgelines, the movement of the stars, if it came to that. I reassured him that I knew about these things. *Hush.* There was the loon again, the flicker. In the room above us, other people were ending their day with all the sounds of undressing (the zippers, the belt buckle hitting the floor), and they had no idea. I told him that all of this was the simple rotation of planets. The rise and fall of magnetism, the surge and retreat of attachment. Wave patterns, dots on the radar. Simple static fanning out across the sky, interrupted, then interrupted, by silence.

He was gone but I moored myself to the boat which
was moored to shore. I crawled from the wooden
berth in the dark of morning and found myself
in the slow-churning mist. The cove was as silent
as the mussels against the shore. Thousands of
jellyfish were blinking and unblinking themselves
like opulent, innocuous little mouths. They pulsed
the surface in soft white pushes and I lowered
myself down the rails of the boat, into the water.
I was naked, awake, and no one knew, but I knew
that ocean, knew it would hold me as I held my
breath, the tide of it pushing back against me.
And outside my skin, the noiseless swirl of tiny
tentacles, the movement of darkness on darkness,
the jellyfish surged because they had to. I was kelp,
I was buoy, and against me, gentle as wings, they
pushed   pushed   pushed.

I awoke one night and he was in the kitchen right at the sink, leaning on the counter with his back to the dirty dishes. He said nothing, just stood there and let me fall into him. The great, dark warmth of him. Cave of chest and neck and chin. I closed my eyes. Trusted his to be open. I stayed there for days. My face was quiet and we said nothing with our mouths. Only our blood could speak: push, push, push.

Then, he was actually there, I saw *(right there)*, papered into me as though we were the same body: hand to mirror hand, chest to mirror chest. As though he never was larger than me, as though, in fact, we were made for this: to fall toward a something, a warm everything, that falls, too; and in falling – it is the blind falling – lands somewhere and stands up for the first time.

When I stood up before him for the first time – the real first time, he was so bright he was blinding, and I could not look him in the face. When I tried I split off, my eyes flashed to the wall, the ceiling, the floor. All I had wanted was his face, and now, I couldn't even bear it, and I bowed my head like submission, like I should bend my knees, leave the pew, and fold my hands before him. (I yielded.) I was solid body and he the ripened light and he was astonished as he stared at me – at me and at the broken light.

Move ahead, I said, *closer to this river so that I can understand what you are singing.* My eyes were incapable against him and my heart was measured against the long passage, and my soul, which was the snow, which was beneath the sun, unsealed.

And I was unsealed before the tidal wave of him that rose toward me, passed over the white sand, threatened in his fearful height to block even the sun. I did not move or seek cover. I did not call out or turn my back and he broke before me and broke into nothing blue or white or ocean grey. Nothing shaped like a tear. He broke into sphere-drops, each one pink and gold and orange. And alive. And impermeable. Unbreakable he that did not land *on* me or *across* me. Did not soak me or knock me off balance, but slowed down and slid through me to impossibly enter my skin and I felt him in all the parts of me where I had forgotten to feel pleasure: he crossed through the skin of my chest, passed through the pink, pulsing organs that sustained me, passed through even the bones of my spine and left me wholly unpunctured. Clean. And in every cell of my being, awake.

He was a black axis. A beautiful swarm. The hollow-boned flight: the birds through a metal tunnel funneling out into a black flock, forming and reforming the images made of their proximity and distance. All space and feathered axis after feathered axis, sometimes flat, sometimes turned to the light, to the horizon, to me.

Into the bulrushes, into the giant talus, into the wheat crop. And I was the empty hive. The egg wash. The straw-headed, diffuse and edgeless. A place where something once lived. And I was the crow blowing over, looking for the waste of him. Waiting to scavenge the ineffable message as it pulsed out of him like radio waves, or a beacon, or an accidental crossbeam of light.

He was bent on rescue, but I had not listened. I was walking through a maze of ancient walls, thinking how lovely a place it was, but he said that the people were looking for us and looking for this thing we had and he had told me to find the certain room and I had gone, but the people there were just sitting around like nothing was coming but dinner. *Is that coming for us?* I asked. *Now?* I asked. And I ran just as the whole wall of glass there exploded and there I was being thrown, sailing through the air with glass in my face and neck and hair. My skin hot from glass and blood. And there was only white silence until there were feet coming through all the dust and bodies and someone had come to collect me: a hand on my shoulder rolled me over and saw that I was still alive – and then it was he that lifted me like a child and carried me off.

He held my arm and guided me through the hallways, up the stairs. Walked me slowly through the crowds of people going other places. He was not the one I wanted to ask for help, but I had gone blind from either pain or vision or the blazing white light or the aperture was broken and it was all blazing light — too bright to take in. I couldn't distinguish the wall from infinity and without him, I was only I in the traffic. And then, all I knew was the hand on my arm, the warmth of a body next to me and I was surprised that he had taken me up. That he was that generous, after all. And I was not fearful. This place was familiar. He showed me the door we were looking for, which was before us, and which I could see now through his eyes. And in seeing was able to find the key among the keys. To turn it. To unlock. To push open.

Then he was gone from his body and floated in blue silver shine that moved and changed, amoebic, before me. I guessed at his color then, imagined it, because really, there was nothing before me. Really, I could not see, nor hear, nor smell, nor taste of him. I could feel only a great solid pressure on me — evenly against me — like a steady, strong wind or a wave of water arriving under water. He was there, pressing into my palms, heavy and doughy in my hands — warm *him* there, giving me some nothing to clutch, some nothing to feed on.

Then one night he floated above me while I slept, but he was not like the faces that appeared and disappeared in the dark of my eyes. He was not the day's memory or tomorrow's plan. I did not even know he was there until some tiny noise in the night house — a small cough or sigh from another room — rose and, as though he was startled, he shattered, fell into me in tiny white shards. He was almost nothing to feel, but my body swelled from

the salt of him and then the I that was not my
body went small inside the great hall of my bones.
And then I left them.

He watched me ride an old bike along the boulevard. I was supposed to be going somewhere else, but the tall gates had been open, so I'd gone there. Fog stirred cool across my knuckles, my knees. I knew the steep hills, the tall brick houses, the solemn lawns. Every earnest porch and door mat was familiar. The wild honeysuckle, the hedge rows. I knew this place, but I didn't know why I knew this place. I coasted beneath the thick maple branches hanging over the curb. It must have been day, but no one was there, and the fog obscured the details.

I thought it was my old home, so I wandered in with tender, reverent steps. Water pitcher, wooden table, framed paintings stared back at me. The stairwell, the windows looked on as though all of this had always been so – but suddenly there were people and this was their house and it was not mine and I hurried to the basement, to the door where my bike rested against the wall. I reached for the knob, but the door opened and they were all in a clutter of talk and the children were carrying on and the mother was not looking. And when she turned, her eyes saw only the room: coats on hooks, boots in a line, an enamel wash basin scrubbed to white.

The four of them came in, walked straight through me, and I felt nothing but dense fog. I walked my bike through the garden in the backyard. No one saw me and no one heard a thing.

In the space of a breath, the scene had split open. The neighborhood parted as though some seam had been loosed and the hundred-year-old oak, the parked cars, the people moving about for evening were opened like an eye opens or like thick curtains open to reveal the true stage – the yellow-gold world behind – while the people carried on, cast in the deep purple grey of appropriate dusk. He was a cut in the canvas open only so briefly. Brilliant, slim light burning through. But it was too soon – it was not yet time. And some quick hand pinned it up. Sewed us back into our single, livable spaces.

He was there after the rain, in the night lawns, thick and arcing, and I could feel him leaving me, falling away from the fabric of human air. Waxy oak leaves let fall a single drop, a single drop: there, gone. Rain-drawn oils rose to the road's surface shine and the silent ghost of old traffic made every sound bright. It must have been late. On the right side of the road, yards sloped down toward houses. Silhouettes showed familiar people in lit windows who drank wine, ate figs and strawberries, and buttered their bread while they laughed together. They waited for me to arrive since I had promised to return. Since I had promised to tell them — had promised him I would tell.

Behind me there was something that used to be important: an old story of false wings and fabricated flights. The streetlamp threw my shadow. Parked cars interrupted the arc of light on the wet road. Something was there that would never leave. I stood still and took in the plain night, smelled the lilacs, the lilies. I let the humid night be just the humid night. The people would wait for me as I had waited. So much had happened and now again I was a body upright: an axis of the turning world. Skull shining. Marrow-glow. Radial bloom.

I was standing in the grass of my own yard. He was gone but not truly absent. He had simply gone ahead of me. He called to me from the distance but I was still moved by the simple ground beneath my feet, green and wild. I wanted to say *I will sing you as no one ever has,* but he already knew and just waited now for his words to surface in me and ride on my voice into the human air. He was far away and my song was small. *Louder,* he called. I heard his echo (echo ring). I leaned forward and opened my mouth to sing.

NOTES

"He stuns you by degrees." Emily Dickinson, [he fumbles at your spirit]. "we come to you directly without touching," Lucille Clifton, "the message from The Ones."

I.

"uncertain longings," "wait for the wind to die down," "fall as a dead body falls," Dante, *Inferno*. Translated by Allen Mandelbaum. "Ein muss sein" *(It must be)*, Milan Kundera, *The Unbearable Lightness of Being*. "Talk low, talk slow and don't say too much." John Wayne

inspired by: "[the soul] leaves the small nest of the body, goes where he wants." *The Upanishads*. "quick now, here, now, always," T. S. Eliot, *Four Quartets*. "I take from you as you take me apart." "Letter to Emily Dickinson," Annie Finch.

II.

"Halloran rhythm" after **Stephen Halloran**, contemporary composer. "brute beauty," **Gerard Manley Hopkins**, "Windhover." "manibus, oh, date lilia plenis," **Dante**, *Purgatorio*, translated by Allen Mandelbaum. "gravity's cold necessity," **Simone Weil**. "the dry stone, no sound of water," **T. S. Eliot**, "The Wasteland." "The dancers are all gone under the hill" "The houses are all gone under the sea." **T. S. Eliot**, *Four Quartets*. "smooth stones, diminishing," **Greta Wrolstad**, "Notes on Sea and Shore." "pale blue cup," James Joyce, *Chamber Music.*

III.

"the movement of darkness on darkness," **T.S. Eliot**, *Four Quartets*. "diamond," **Gerard Manley Hopkins**, "That Nature is a Heraclitean Fire and of the Comfort of the Resurrection." "astonished as [they] stared at me – at me and at the broken light," Dante, *Purgatorio.* "move ahead, and closer to this river so that I may understand what you are singing." *Purgatorio.* "measured by the longing to receive it [grace]," *Paradiso.* "I yield, I am defeated at this passage," *Paradiso.* "so is the snow, beneath the sun, unsealed," *Paradiso.* Translated by Allan Mandelbaum. "beacon [...] crossbeam of light," Gerard Manley Hopkins. "I will sing you as no one ever has." R.M. Rilke, *Book of Hours*. Translated by Anita Barrows and Joanne Macy.

ABOUT THE AUTHOR

Amy Ratto Parks is the author of *How to Remember the World* (forthcoming, fall 2018), *Song of Days, Torn and Mended,* and *Bread and Water Body,* winner of the Merriam Frontier Chapbook Prize. Her poems have appeared in *Mid-American Review, Interim, Mikrokosmos, The Mississippi Review, Court Green,* and *Barrow Street* among others. Ratto Parks has worked as a reporter, a freelance writer and online writing course designer, and an editor of *Writer's Digest, Fiction Writer,* and *Cutbank*. She currently teaches at the University of Montana.

ABOUT THE PRESS

Since 2008, Folded Word has been
exploring the world, one voice at a time
with the help of editors, authors, and readers
who value sustainable literature.

For a complete list of our titles, visit the Folded Word website: FOLDED.WORDPRESS.COM

To report typographical errors, email: FoldedEditors@gmail.com

Want more information about our titles? Want to connect with our authors? No problem. Simply join us at a social media outlet near you:

- Facebook:www.facebook.com/foldedword
- Twitter: twitter.com/foldedword

FOLDED WORD

is a proud member of

[clmp]

Community of Literary Magazines and Presses

Ensuring a vibrant, diverse literary landscape

www.clmp.org

and gives annual support to:

Poets House

A place for poetry: library, literary center, locus of poetic inspiration

poetshouse.org

The Haiku Foundation

Preserving and archiving the first century of haiku in English; providing resources for the next

www.thehaikufoundation.org

WHAT DID YOU THINK?

Let us know with a quick rating or review at
GoodReads.com
or wherever you search for books.

Folded Word reserves a portion of each print run to donate to libraries and reading programs in under-served communities. Please email us at FoldedEditors@gmail.com if you would like your organization to be considered.

COLOPHON

This book and its cover were designed and typeset by JS Graustein, featuring her abstract photograph "Fog Horizon."

The title face is Festivo LC, designed and issued by Ahmet Altun in 2014.

The subtitle face is Tropical Brush, designed by Joluvian and Alejandro Paul in 2017, issued by Sudtipos.

The text face and supplemental glyphs are Paciencia, designed by Thiago Oliveira in 2017, issued by Typographias.

Printed in the United States of America by Walch Printing of Portland, Maine, on 70# Cougar Natural, an acid-free, FSC® Certified, SFI® Certified Sourcing, and Rainforest Alliance Certified™ sustainable paper.